THE LONDON ZOO

SALLY HOLLOWAY

Folio Miniatures

MICHAEL JOSEPH
London

FOLIO MINIATURES
General Editor: John Letts

First published in Great Britain by
Michael Joseph Ltd
52 Bedford Square
London WC1B 3EF
1976

© *1976 Sally Holloway*

ISBN 0 7181 1475 2

ACKNOWLEDGEMENTS

In offering this book on the 150th anniversary of the foundation of
the Zoological Society of London, I would like to express my sincere
thanks to Miss Eirwen Owen, CBE, the Director of Administration of
the Society, and to Dr H. Gwynne Vevers, MBE, DPhil, FLS, FI Biol;
to Prof E. J. W. Barrington, MA, DSc, FRS; to Mr R. A. Fish, FLA and
to the staff of the Society's library, all of whom have helped very
considerably with my work.

S.E.H.
London 1976

All the pictures in the book, including the endpaper, showing an
early entrance ticket to the London Zoo, are by kind permission of
the Zoological Society except the following: page 31 The Illustrated
London News; page 28 Cedric Price and Frank Newby; pages 34
and 35 The National Portrait Gallery, London.

PRINTED AND BOUND IN BELGIUM
by Henri Proost & Cie p.v.b.a., Turnhout

The Zoological Society of London . . . for the advancement of Zoology and Animal Physiology, and the introduction of new and curious subjects of the Animal Kingdom . . .

extract from the Royal Charter granted
by George IV in 1829

The concept of a Zoological Society for London was launched into the fashionable world of the 1820s in the earnest hope that it would bear the same relation to the developing science of Zoology as that which the Horticultural Society already bore to botany and the vegetable kingdom.

The instant reaction was ridicule. In London salons, wits christened it 'The Noah's Ark Society'. *The Literary Gazette*, the journal of the day devoted to science and literature, wrote:

'It has been much canvassed and we hear a great diversity of opinions upon it. Those friendly to it . . . declare it to be worthy of an enlightened country and anticipate wonderful improvements from its being carried into effect, whilst those of an opposite way of thinking laugh at it as wild speculation and con little thanks to the President of the Royal Society for attempting to make an Ark in London for the reception of pairs of living things after their kinds.'

The idea was dismissed as 'too visionary', but Sir Stamford Raffles and the Royal Society's President, Sir Humphrey Davy, were already determined to go ahead on their course and neither was the type of man to be diverted by shallow criticism.

As early as 1817 Thomas Stamford Raffles, brilliant amateur naturalist, anthropologist and founder (through his employers, the East India Company) of Singapore, had nursed the idea of a Society devoted solely to the animal world. He had built up an immense personal knowledge of animals and plants, particularly from the Malayan Archipelago, and had a private collection of specimens large enough in itself to start a small museum.

In 1825, a year after his final return to England from the Far East, Raffles came to be appointed Chairman of a committee set up by 'friends of the proposed Zoological Society'. Many of them had been or still were members of the Linnean Society of naturalists but wanted to diversify from the strict lines laid down by the Zoological Club of the Linnaeans.

Raffles accepted the position and in 1825 wrote to his cousin, Dr Thomas Raffles: 'I am much interested at present in establishing a Grand Zoological Collection in the Metropolis. We expect to have 20,000 subscribers at £2 each and it is further expected that we may go far beyond the Jardin des Plantes at Paris. Sir Humphrey Davy and myself are the projectors and while he looks more to the practical and immediate utility to the country gentleman, my attention is more directed to the scientific department.'

Davy, inventor of the miners' safety lamp and a comfortably-off country gentleman himself, was anxious to find new types or breeds of animals and birds which might prosper on country estates, as well as to improve existing strains.

Accordingly, the aims of the Society, laid down in its first prospectus in July 1825, were for 'the introduction of new varieties, breeds and races of animals for the purposes of domestication or for stocking our farm-yards, woods, pleasure grounds and waters, with the establishment of a general Zoological Collection consisting of prepared specimens in the different classes and orders, so as to afford a correct view of the Animal Kingdom at large in as complete a series as may be practicable . . .'.

Those who wished to be an original member of the new Society would pay an annual subscription of £2 and an admission fee of £3.

The scheme, despite its critics, was an instant success. Charles Bell and Everard Home, both distinguished anatomists, Robert Peel the Home Secretary, the Duke of Bedford, the

4

Marquess of Lansdowne, the Earl of Lonsdale and an assortment of MPs were among the original 131 subscribers.

The project of a park or garden containing living animals soon expanded to include a museum and a library 'of all Books connected with the subject'. A committee of 'Noblemen and Gentlemen' was set up to administer the Society and its proposed Gardens and this was to set the tone which made the Zoo almost exclusively the playground of the rich for its first decade.

Keeping wild animals in captivity was not new. Henry of Huntingdon wrote in his 'Latin Chronicle' of 1110: 'Henry I was extremely fond of the wonders of distant countries, taking with great delight from foreign Kings, Lions, Leopards, Lynxes and Camels, animals which England does not produce. He has a park called Woodstock in which he used to foster favourites of this kind . . . .'

Henry III founded the Royal Menagerie at the Tower of London after being presented with three leopards by his brother-in-law, the Emperor Frederick II. A manuscript of the College of Arms at the time says: 'Since the arrival of three leopards in London in 1250 there are constant records of payment made for the maintenance of the animals at the Tower.' In 1255 the Sheriffs of London 'were desired to build a house for the elephant sent to Henry III by Louis IX of France'. This was the first elephant seen in England and these animals formed the basis of the long-famous Tower Menagerie.

The Gardens of the Zoological Society were to be different. These were not just animals for show but a display aimed at being not only a source of study in its own right but a means of raising enough money to support scientific research.

The newly established committee, later to become the Council of the Society, set to work quickly. A title was agreed: 'The Zoological Society of London' (it never became 'Royal' despite its early Charter from George IV), and application was made to the Government for a suitable piece of ground in Regent's Park. Although the central position the Society had hoped for was not forthcoming they were offered another portion to the north and close by the Canal. Raffles and his colleagues inspected it and found it would be by no means ideal. The soil was clay, drainage would be a problem and the site was already bisected by the Outer Circle, the ring road round the Park. There was more correspondence but finally the Society was granted a plot of land comprising five acres at an annual rent of £6. 6/- per acre and 8/- a foot on the road frontage, on a yearly tenancy. This was accepted and the Society held its first full meeting in the house of the Horticultural Society in Regent Street on 29th April, 1826. It was attended by forty-eight members and Sir Stamford Raffles was formally appointed President. He then read the first Presidential Address, a review of the past and present state of Zoology in the country. £5,000 was set aside for the Gardens and a further £1,000 for a museum. The Society had begun.

It could not have been more propitiously timed. The great era of Victorian expansion was already beginning; the Empire was blossoming and seething with wildlife; steam power was becoming a practical possibility, speeding the ships which brought precious and fragile live specimens across the world. Only one event marred the prospect. Within three months of its foundation the Society lost its President. Sir Stamford Raffles was only forty-four years old when he suddenly died of apoplexy following a brain tumour on 5th July, 1826.

Despite this, the cause was flourishing and within months membership had risen to 300. A headquarters was set up at 33 Bruton Street, W1, and not only humans passed through its austere doors. Already, news of the Society had spread and living specimens were arriving, embarrassingly at times, as the harassed staff found when on one occasion a visiting bishop had his wig whisked off by a newly-donated Wanderoo monkey.

Work on the Gardens was due to begin and Decimus Burton, who designed much of Kew Gardens, was invited to submit plans. While he did so, a small museum was opened in

The Wanderoo Monkey (from the 'Zoological Gardens delineated', published in 1830)

the Bruton Street offices and an unheard-of step was taken by the Council. It was resolved that ladies be admitted as members on the same terms as men. Lady Raffles, widow of Sir Stamford, was the first. Later, she presented his whole collection of specimens to the Society's Museum.

Despite such promising enlightenment, the Zoological Society was and would remain for many years almost exclusively the pleasure ground of the rich. Its foundation had depended on them; its initial purpose was to prosper their estates and it was through this elite that, initially at least, it was so successful. As early as 1827 the Foreign Office co-operated by sending out a circular from the Society to its representatives all over the world, filling in the blanks appropriately:

'SIR, – I take the liberty, with the sanction of . . ., of sending to you the last report of the Zoological Society.

It is possible that in the course of your residence at . . . opportunities of promoting our views and objects may occur to you and that you may be able to send us occasionally, and at very inconsiderable expense, specimens of subjects of Zoology of much curiosity and interest.

'Living specimens of all rare animals and particularly of such as may possibly be domesticated and become useful here, will be much valued by us; and above all, varieties of the deer kind, and of gallinaceous birds; but beyond this, preserved insects, reptiles, birds, mammalia, fishes, eggs and shells will be gratefully received.

'And I may mention that where a more scientific method does not occur, the promiscuous immersion of any number of subjects in a tub of strong brine (feathers, bodies and all) will be sufficient for preservation, not quite effectual, perhaps, for the skins in all instances but perfectly so for the purposes of dissection and comparative anatomy.'

On 27th April, 1828 the Gardens of what we know today as the London Zoo were opened to the public for the first time, although entrance was restricted to members only and their guests. (It was not until 1847, when the gate money fell disastrously, that the Society was forced unwillingly, by financial stringency, to widen its gates and admit *hoi polloi* at 1/- a head and 6d on Mondays.)

Decimus Burton's earliest plan shows the site bisected, as it is today, by the Outer Circle. As soon as the gardens were laid out and the first buildings erected, the fashionable set which had laughed at the idea of a Noah's Ark Society was happy enough to pour through its gates and marvel at such delights as the Llama House, the large aviary, one or two small houses and the pond which comprised the whole of the Zoo in that first year. By its end, 98,000 people had come to see the earliest inmates, who included a Griffon Vulture called Dr Brookes (which lived in the Zoo for forty years), a white-

8

The tunnel, built by Decimus Burton in 1830 (from the Martin Duncan Collection)

headed eagle and a small female deer.

Animals had to be cared for and the first of the Zoo keepers wore a top hat, bottle green coat, striped waistcoat and breeches tucked into Wellington boots with painted tops.

Already, society was inspired by the dream of Zoology and the upper classes poured in money and reached out through all their spheres of influence to encourage so worthy a cause.

The Hudson's Bay Company, the East India Company, the Asiatic Society of Calcutta, officers of the Army and the Royal Navy, gentlemen and even ladies rushed to help. Enthusiasm was so great that a new class of Corresponding Members was instituted by the Society to embrace amateur zoologists from all the outposts of the Empire.

By 1829 the King, George IV, had come under the spell and was persuaded to grant a Royal Charter under the title 'The Zoological Society of London . . . for the advancement of Zoology and Animal Physiology, and the introduction of new and curious subjects of the Animal Kingdom . . .'.

It must have seemed that new and curious subjects were arriving by every ship that furled its sails in the ports of England. Although few of Decimus Burton's original plans were carried out (partly because of the bickering which was to continue within the Council of the Society for many years to come, partly from lack of financial resources) and the northern half of the Gardens was not developed until some time later, his tunnel joining the two halves below the road was built and some houses erected, including his superb aviary in which the pillars supporting the roof were designed to look like the trunks of palm trees. His plan for the Carnivora House was a graceful building with open air yards for the animals in front of their dens. Council members doubted whether animals from foreign climes should be exposed to the damp and mists of Regent's Park. Damp it certainly was. Drainage was a constant problem and at one time many animals, particularly monkeys, died of pulmonary diseases including tuberculosis. Battle was joined between the advocates of open air against those who favoured indoor heat. The latter won and for many years the lions, tigers and monkeys as well as visitors suffered from the hot, stuffy, odorous buildings. Finally, the open-air advocates rallied again and triumphed. The Carnivora House was eventually turned into a museum and the lions and tigers had a new home.

There were, however, from the earliest days, an outdoor Bear Pit and Bears' Terrace, which became a popular attraction, and an assortment of houses and dens which appear to have been built on a multi-purpose basis to accommodate, if only temporarily, whatever animals the next high tide might bring in. There was no shortage. In 1830 William IV handed over all the animals from the Royal Menagerie at Windsor Park, including four goats, two llamas, thirteen kangaroos, four zebras, three gnus, four macaws, two cockatoos, eleven emus, forty-two peafowl (assorted) and seven coreopsis geese. The following year he added the contents of the Tower Menagerie including one hundred rattlesnakes and an Indian elephant. Hopes were expressed that the armadillo 'so valuable as an article of food' might be naturalised.

More staff were taken on – keepers and gardeners – and a system of Daily Occurrence Sheets started on 25th February, 1828, which are still produced. The first reported: 'eleven wild duck received for the Lake; six silver haired rabbits from Mr Blake; an otter has died from a diseased tail; an emu has laid her 4th egg. All animals and birds well. Servants all on duty. Number of visitors: four. Particular Visitors: Lord Auckland.'

The whole question of rearing animals and experimenting with breeding, which had been particularly in Davy's mind in setting up the Zoo, was now becoming a problem. The cages were filling fast but crowds were pouring in too, baiting the bears and chattering all day round the dens and cages so that the background was anything but a peaceful setting suitable for procreation.

After a great deal of discussion, the Council decided that a quieter venue must be sought for this. (Whipsnade was the final solution but not for another century.) In 1829 the Society negotiated with the Corporation of Kingston and a Mr Pallmer, the local MP, for 'the occupation of a farm . . . with some 33 acres of land . . . in a beautiful situation under the wall of Richmond Park, with a light soil peculiarly favourable for rearing birds, full of very abundant springs and with some excellent ponds'. This was some eleven miles from London and while Fellows and Friends had access, it was not so easy to drop in on casually as the central Regent's Park. Davy's dream of producing stock for gentlemen's estates was still a prime aim of the Society and in 1831 its Committee of Science and Correspondence reported on their efforts to introduce 'animals for domestication, likely to supply the objects of food, clothing, medicine or draft', including 'deer, antelope, turkeys, guinea fowls, the Struthious Birds, Curassows, Penelopes etc.'

Turkeys, curassows and penelopes might have been over-ambitious. By 1832 it was suggested that Fellows of the Society could be offered specimens of the rarer kinds of pigeons, rabbits, or domestic fowl of variegated silver and Chinese pheasants from the farm. There was also a suggestion that 'kangaroos, emus, black swans and Capercaily [sic], Norwegian grouse and bustard' might be bred there.

Animal physiology was always a controversial subject and the farm was not without its background of storms. Some members became incensed at the mention of such possibilities as cross-hybridisation and this, coupled with the undoubted fact that the majority of them preferred to enjoy their animals at leisure in attractive and easily accessible surroundings, had its effect. The farm was given up in 1834.

The museum was another short-lived enterprise of the early days. Not only were enthusiastic hunters sending back live animals but they had reacted energetically to the suggestion that dead specimens would also be welcomed. So many arrived that the Society's small museum was overwhelmed. New premises were taken in Leicester Square but these, too were swiftly outgrown and for a time all the contents were stored in a warehouse at Golden Square until the original Carnivora House was turned into a museum within the Gardens. Eventually, in 1855, the Zoo Council decided that the British Museum's Natural History Section, which at one time had been in a very poor state, was now sufficiently well organised and established to make their own an expensive luxury. Its contents were divided up. Some went to the Natural History Museum, some to the Museum of Trinity College, Dublin, and the rest to help foster the now rapidly growing interest in Zoology in provincial universities and museums.

While it lasted the museum was the particular favourite of

Nicholas Aylward Vigors, the first Secretary of the Society. It was through him that John Gould was appointed Curator and Preserver to the Museum. Gould, one of the most illustrious of British naturalists, was a skilled taxidermist, married to a talented artist. By 1832 he had begun to produce a series of folios, starting with 'A century of Birds from the Himalaya Mountains', followed by 'Birds of Europe', 'A Monograph of the Toucans', volumes on the Trogons and more. He only resigned from his post to go to Australia where he produced another massive work, 'Birds of Australia'. He died many years later, in 1881, but it was the Society which gave him the first opportunity to develop his remarkable talents.

By the mid 1830s the Society was flourishing. Davy's influence, which, perhaps, had predominated at first, was giving way to Raffles's direction and the various scientific sections were by now well-established and thriving. Lectures on all the known aspects of animal sciences were given regularly by most of the leading zoologists of the time and these were reproduced in the Society's publications, either

'The Transactions of the Zoological Society of London', or in 'The Proceedings'. Progress in zoology was recorded from the mid 1860s in 'The Zoological Record', which continues today and remains indispensable to the zoologist.

Although the Society began long before photographic representations of the specimens could be produced, the Council employed a series of artists to paint the more scientifically important, as a whole and in anatomical detail. Among the first 'Zoo' artists was Edward Lear and one is tempted to believe that this part of his life, when lists of strange animals were before him every day with such names as struthious birds, whiskered yarkes, cassowaries, aye-ayes, gallinules, penelopes, quaggas, jerfalcons, francolins and magapodius, must have lingered in his mind and emerged later, translated into the strange creatures of his Nonsense verse.

Thomas Landseer, brother of Sir Edwin, was another famous zoo artist and so also was the outstanding Joseph Wolf, who later gave several sets of his animal studies to the Zoo library. Their clear, detailed watercolours of animals, birds and reptiles were bound into the earliest record books and are now among the treasured archives.

One of the more interesting as well as the earliest of Lear's paintings shows *Felis Leo Goojratensis* – the Maneless Lion of Guzerat. It was reproduced from one of two skins presented to the Society by Captain Walter Smee of the Bombay Army in 1828. In a lecture to members he explained that this was an extremely rare animal and he had shot eleven males and females himself. It could, he thought, have been one of the race of lions without manes mentioned by Pliny and also the same maneless lion which occurs in the older armorial bearings of England.

Among the later fine collections of animal drawings presented to the Zoo was the complete set of bird studies made by Major Henry Jones, FZS, a devoted amateur ornithologist. These too, are preserved in the Library.

By the early 1830s a constant stream of animals was pouring in and every effort was made then, and throughout the

Society's history, to see that they were all treated on their journeys in a way most likely to ensure their safety and comfort.

One of the earlier documents surviving in the records is an instruction to those despatching animals that they should be 'domesticated as far as possible . . . correspondents should engage some individual of the ship's company to take charge of the Animals on board and guarantee to him a handsome recompense on bringing them safely to their destination. . .'. Food was important on these journeys, not least for birds, and again correspondents were advised: 'Ants' eggs, which are abundant in tropical climates, may be preserved in a jar, well tied down and with the addition of the *Blattae* or cock-roaches so generally attainable on board ship in all their stages of growth, and of meal worms which are equally abundant in the bread room. . . .'

By 1831 the Gardens could list among its inmates 'wolves, hyenas, lions, tigers, chittahs [*sic*], puma, ocelot, panthers, apes, spider monkeys, lemurs, armadillo, zebra, deer, antelope, goats, sheep, kangaroo, squirrels, beaver, porcupines, vultures, eagles, falcons, owls' as well as 'assorted birds, including parrots, parrakeets, macaws, cockatoos, storks, crane, heron and pelican'.

It was an impressive list and in 1832, the following year, an auction had to be held when fifty 'lots' of superfluous animals were sold. Yet scientists needed more creatures though of different varieties. Rare specimens, not yet received as gifts, began to be sought individually.

In 1833 the Council negotiated through Colonel Campbell, HM Consul General in Egypt, for a M Thibaut 'to proceed to Nubia for the purpose of procuring a Giraffe on the Society's account'. The terms appear sharp if not harsh, but M Thibaut seems to have accepted them, although no cash was to be paid until he delivered the animals alive and well to Malta. His vivid report of his hunt through the desert in company with a band of Arab tribesmen gives an insight into the background to the capture of the creatures upon which the Victorian

The Polar Bear (from 'Zoological Gardens', pub. Dean & Munday c 1835)

public gazed open-mouthed and through which their scientists built their foundations of knowledge.

Thibaut collected five giraffes altogether, resting for three or four days at a time to make them sufficiently tame to travel on through the desert. 'During this period an Arab constantly holds it at the end of a long cord,' he explained in his report. 'By degrees it becomes accustomed to the presence of man and takes a little nourishment'. He brought his party, complete with giraffes, back to Kordofan but four of the young animals died in the cold winter and he was forced to return for three months before he finally captured a further trio. Even then, as he wrote, 'another trial was reserved for me; that of transporting the animals by bark from Wadi Halfa to Cairo, Alexandria and Malta. Providence has enabled me to surmount all difficulties. The most that they suffered was at sea during the passage which lasted 24 days with the weather very tempestuous.' The giraffes wintered in Malta so that they might

The Monkey House (from 'Zoological Gardens', pub. Dean & Munday c 1835)

become acclimatised and they were then brought to London, where they walked from the Docks to Regent's Park in a solemn procession which delighted the crowds who welcomed them along the route. A special house had been prepared for them and, said the Council Report, 'the safe arrival of four of these rare and beautiful animals in Regent's Park on the 24th May, 1836 has formed an era in the history of the Society highly creditable to its resources and to its zeal in promoting one of the leading objects for which the Society was established. It is no less encouraging to be able to add that the expenses attendant on their importation have been fully defrayed by the increased attraction afforded by their exhibition in the Menagerie.' One died in January 1837 but the remaining three lived on in good health. The female gave birth to seven calves before dying in 1852 and the progeny of the group kept the Zoo stocked with giraffes until 1881.

There were similar adventures when, in the 1850s, the

Society sought a hippopotamus. Abbay Pasha, Viceroy of Egypt, sent a party of special hunters to the White Nile, where they managed to capture a three-day old baby hippo off the Isle of Obaysch. It was escorted back by a company of infantry: 'By the obliging and liberal co-operation of the Peninsular and Oriental Company an apparatus was constructed on board the steamer *Ripon* by which the peculiar requirements of the animal were perfectly accommodated.' On 25th May, 1850 the first living hippopotamus since the tertiary period was landed on English soil. A special train brought him to London and crowds gathered at every wayside station to gaze at the monster – though fruitlessly, since according to a contemporary report 'they only saw the Arab keeper who . . . for want of air, was constrained to put his head out through the roof'. The hippo was named Obaysch and his arrival produced even more uproar than the giraffes. Visitors rose from 168,000 in 1849 to 360,000 in 1850. In 1853 a mate, Adhela, was bought for Obaysch and a new hippo house built. The Arab attendant, Hamet Saafi Canaani, stayed on to look after them; for the first time London was struck by a new form of dementia – hippomania. There were hippo songs, hippo verses, and even sheet music for a Hippopotamus Polka. Obaysch lived on in the Gardens for twenty-nine years.

New houses were now being built almost every year and not only for the animals. The need for overall supervision was recognised early and a Superintendent's House was built in 1838. At first the head of the Gardens was a man interested in animal welfare but gradually the scientific importance of the post was realised and eventually in 1904 it was taken over by fully qualified zoologists. As the demand for more keepers was made, they began to be employed from outside, but at first they lived on the premises, usually over the giraffes.

In 1834 the famous Carnivora Terrace was opened and this rapidly became the fashionable Sunday promenade for London society. By 1839 there was a new large Monkey House and in 1840 new external cages were added in the hope that fresh air might stop the spread of tuberculosis among the inmates. By 1844 there was a polar bears' den with an enclosure and bath.

Although science was now overtaking the needs of the estates of country gentlemen, efforts were still being made to maintain this aspect of the Society's foundation. In 1844 the Council established premiums for the various descriptions of poultry and announced improvements in several breeds of domestic animals.

By now the century was half through and the Zoological Gardens had become not only the world centre of animal study but a fashionable retreat, particularly on Sundays. Access was still restricted to Fellows and their friends on this one day and parents brought their offspring along not so much to study Zoology as in the hope of finding them suitable marriage partners.

Arrangements for tickets had changed through the years and Fellows (successors to the original 'members') were now able to buy books of tickets, some of which were illegally exchanged for drink in nearby public houses so that the company which found its way through the gates on Sundays was not always as suitable as the Society would have wished. A newspaper article of the period commented: 'Fellows' tickets are remarkably apt to work their way downwards and the two or three thousand people who . . . find their way here on a Sunday afternoon comprise a good many from all classes . . . many of the regular habitués of the place see very little of [the animals]. They lounge and gossip and quiz the passers-by or promenade up and down and show their dresses.'

In 1867, a musical-hall artist, the Great Vance, coined a new word and the Gardens of the Zoological Society suddenly became 'The Zoo' for the first time. The snob importance of belonging to the Society is clear in the chorus of his song 'Walking in the Zoo':

The OK thing to do
On Sunday afternoon
Is to toddle to the Zoo.
Week-days may do for cads,
But not for me and you,
So dress'd right down the road
We show them who is who.
The Walking in the Zoo
Is the OK thing on Sunday.

But while the fashionable spurned the contents of the cages for other attractions, the everyday visitors still poured in to see the new arrivals, whether they were individual characters like 'Tommy' the first chimpanzee, who had travelled from Bristol to London by stage-coach with his keeper, or the great collections from the Empire. The giraffes, the hippos and later the anteaters all produced surging record gates. So too did the great Royal Collections.

Gifts from the Royal Family had arrived regularly, often depending on visits from foreign heads of state and occasionally on royal journeys abroad. Queen Victoria had become Patroness of the Society on her accession in 1837 and Prince Albert was President from 1851 until his death. During the whole of this period they had given animals, but in 1876 the Prince of Wales (later King Edward VII) paid a State Visit to India and not only deposited the whole of the animal collection he had accrued on the journey to be cared for by the Society but presented them with two tigers, two leopards and an elephant, two antelopes and two tragopans. Receipts rocketed and the following year the Prince was presented with the Society's Gold Medal.

Occasionally, surprising events brought in big crowds and one of the most remarkable of these was Jumbomania.

'Jumbo' was the first African elephant to be kept in the Zoo. He was exchanged for a rhino with the Jardin des Plantes in Paris and soon developed into an enormous animal, 11 feet 6 inches tall and weighing $6\frac{1}{2}$ tons. His temperament was never dependable. He constantly smashed up the timber of his den and snapped off the tips of both his tusks in the process. Eventually he contracted enteric fever and when he was at the point of death his keeper, Matthew Scott, asked permission to take over his treatment. The Council of the Society agreed. Scott was a strange character and although he had been awarded the Society's Bronze Medal for his work in rearing animals he had also been at the centre of an over-publicised incident in which it was suggested that he had saved the lives of two fellow keepers when a rhinoceros attacked them. Whatever the truth of this, there seems no doubt that Scott saved Jumbo's life, albeit by unorthodox methods. He lived and slept with the elephant day and night, talked to it constantly and willed it to survive. For medicine he produced a nightly bucket of whisky. Jumbo recovered but was now Scott's devoted slave. Fellows visiting the Gardens with their ladies found Scott arrogant and offensive. Their complaints embarrassed the Zoo Council but no other keeper could go near the giant beast.

There was more. Jumbo and his master turned their 'medicine' into a regular nightly tonic, Scott slipping out for his 'dram' and returning with a bucket for his charge. Finally salvation appeared in the shape of a representative from Barnum's Circus in America. The Zoo Council was prepared to let Jumbo go for £2,000 provided Barnum's was responsible for his transport. They had not anticipated the public outrage which was to follow, almost certainly stimulated by the subtle publicity methods of Phineas T. Barnum. Londoners rose and demanded that Jumbo must stay. The press discovered that there was a female elephant, Alice, and claimed that she was Jumbo's adoring wife who would be heartbroken if he were shipped across the ocean. Protest reached riot proportions and there were questions in Parliament before Jumbo was finally exported across the Atlantic. Although the matter was touched on only briefly in the annual reports of the Council of the Society, who claimed that Jumbo was potentially dangerous (a curious argument if they were prepared to allow him to be let loose on the public in an open circus ring), it brought another rush of visitors and near record 'gates'.

Tragically, Jumbo's circus life lasted only three years. In 1885 he wandered from the circus train into the path of the Grand Trunk Express Freighter at St Thomas, Ontario. He died an hour later, his trunk wrapped round the hand of the heartbroken Matthew Scott.

It was only after they had gone that the Zoo discovered that Scott had been charging the public for elephant rides. They took this over themselves, and charging 2d a head for elephant and camel rides made a regular £500 a year.

All that remained of Jumbo was his name, which would be used from then on to describe anything of similar massive proportions, and his hide, which was stuffed and used by Barnum as an articulated model.

The sheer physical problem of looking after so many and varied animals and birds was one which the Society had to review constantly. The health of the inmates was a problem too, since there were no precedents and every effort made in care and rearing must, of necessity, be on a trial and error basis. The Reptile House, built in 1849 and the first in the world, produced enormous problems of hygiene. (It was said that cockroaches, which bred in the humidity of the steam pipes beneath its dens, became a useful source of food for other animals.)

One of the earliest major losses caused by lack of experience was the first baby giraffe to be born to the female brought back from Egypt by M Thibaut. There was so much human attention at its birth that the mother rejected it and it was fed by hand on cow's milk, but in such strength that it died when only a few days old. Keepers and zoologists compared notes and realised above all that they should have left the mother alone to cope with the birth. When the next calf was due, the keepers stayed well away, the mother accepted her baby, suckled it and reared it to become a healthy adult.

Accommodation, where the whole question of housing animals away from their natural homes was concerned, was equally a matter of trial and error and conditions in the Gardens were often poor and occasionally squalid. At first scientists recognised no connection between scientific investigation and the treatment of animals, although as early as 1829 a 'medical attendant' from Camden Town nearby was appointed at £60 per annum 'to attend three times in each week and oftener when necessary to prescribe for and examine all animals and to keep a record of his observations and practice'. By 1833 a medical superintendent, a Mr W. Youatt, was appointed at £100 a year and he was provided with a room to make post-mortem examinations. Much later the Zoo began a long co-operative association with the nearby Royal Veterinary College.

In 1865 Professor T. H. Huxley urged that better use should be made of the bodies of dead animals for research and as a result a Zootomical Committee was set up and a 'dead-house' and dissecting room built. A 'Prosector' was appointed whose duty was to examine all animals who died in the Gardens, write up reports on them and dispose of the bodies according to the Council's instructions. The value of these animals to medical science has been immense. Early surgeons, including Sir Arthur Keith, Sir Frederick Treves and Sir John Bland-Sutton, were among those whose research was helped by dissecting animals which had died in the Zoo. Subjects ranged across the whole medical spectrum from muscle and bone structure to tonsils and heart disease. Yet although so much work was done on carcasses, at no time in its history has the Society allowed any of its animals to be used for vivisection.

(In addition to the Prosectorship, a system of five-year Anatomical Research Fellowships was set up in 1926 to provide facilities for young anatomists. One of the first of these was awarded to Dr S. Zuckerman, a graduate of Capetown University who later became a distinguished Honorary Secretary of the Society.)

But the work of the Zoo was not confined strictly to Regent's Park and by the 1880s it was not only encouraging and advising those who wanted to set up new Zoos all over the world but had helped to establish the internationally famous Marine Biological Association at Plymouth. Later, grants were made to expeditions comprising scientists rather than hunters – £200 to the National Antarctic Expedition, £50 to an expedition to Gambia and, in a different field, £100 towards the expense of preparing the gigantic 'Index Animalium'.

It was at the turn of the century that the work on animal anatomy which had occupied so much of the research in the 1800s began to give way to new lines of thought, and in the years to come it would spread into the fields of comparative biology, biochemistry, radiology, animal physiology, veterinary medicine and comparative medical research; spread, in fact, until by the 1970s the case for retaining Zoology as a science in its own right was beginning to be questioned.

The Zoo had expanded steadily from its original five acres, but not without problems, and at times there were bitter altercations with nearby residents, not least during long hot summers when raw effluent from the cages was discharged into the canal. By the earliest years of the 20th Century the fortunes of both the Gardens and of the Society itself were at a low ebb. Administration was not at its best and although scientists still valued all the Gardens had to offer, it seemed that, for a time at least, the public had lost interest.

In 1903 a Committee of Enquiry which had been set up to look into the declining affairs of the Society presented its Report. It covered almost every branch of the activities and revealed some of the abuses which had been going on for many years as well as an assortment of curious 'perks'. Profits from the Guide to the Gardens had been the property of the Secretary, while the proceeds from the ladies' lavatories belonged, by tradition, to the Superintendent's family. These 'privileges' were abolished. Members of the staff were forbidden to deal in animals. A new Superintendent was appointed, professional auditors were employed to examine the accounts periodically and the system of granting honorary and free admission tickets was revised. In August 1903 a new

Secretary took over – P. Chalmers Mitchell – and during the next few years dramatic changes took place as the whole basis of the Society and its Gardens was reorganised. By 1911 the Zoo was on its feet again and preparing houses for another collection of animals sent to King George V, this time as a gift from South Africa. With this attraction, in 1912 a record number of one million visitors passed through the gates. Enthusiasm was returning.

By now a new breed of benefactor was offering support. In the same year Mr J. Newton Mappin, head of Mappin & Webb, the London jewellers, offered to present 'an installation for the panoramic display of wild animals'. Until this time they had been displayed in cages or, at best, in outdoor paddocks, but during the early 1900s a German animal dealer and circus trainer, Carl Hagenbeck, had begun to advocate that animals were best kept in as near natural surroundings as possible. His gardens near Hamburg had animals in what appeared to be theatrical scenery – and they thrived. It was with this type of structure in mind that the Society and Mr Mappin approached two architects, Mr John Belcher, RA and Mr J. J. Joass, to draw up a similar design for London. The result was a completely revolutionary home for goats, bears and an assortment of animals which could thrive indoors or out.

The new complex, named the Mappin Terraces, was built of ferro-concrete to give the appearance of natural rock with a hollow interior to allow more space. 'The hills will be modelled to represent natural scenery; the enclosures for the bears will represent massive Roman architecture . . . the lower and more formal portions, the steps giving access to the Terraces and the Tea Pavilion will recall Italian Renaissance designs,' promised the Zoo Council.

Mr Mappin, a Fellow of the Society, died soon after work began on the Terraces. By the time they were finished, the First World War had begun.

Despite this, the Zoo continued to attract crowds, particularly after the patriotic gesture was made which admitted soldiers and their families at reduced rates.

Meeting of the Zoological Society at Hanover Square by Henry Furniss, published in 1885

Re-building went on steadily in the Gardens until 1926, when the Society began again to think of extending, particularly with a view to keeping animals in larger family groups than was possible in cages and using these to study and experiment with breeding and behaviour. It was much the same argument which had been used, but for a different purpose, over Kingston, and this time the aim was to add to the whole knowledge of this aspect of science and reproduction. It was unlikely that they would be allowed to encroach again into Regent's Park, now a great 'lung' in the centre of London. Instead, they looked further afield. The ideal site would be unlike the existing Gardens which were set in clay, and low-lying. The 480-acre Hall Farm at Whipsnade, thirty miles north-west of London, set high on Dunstable Downs, was more to their taste. It was examined, approved, plans were laid out and put into force and on 31st May, 1930, Whipsnade Zoo was opened to provide the most natural conditions possible for keeping wild animals in captivity.

It was an instant success, both with the public who wanted an interesting day out in the country and as a source of scientific study. Whipsnade has been thriving ever since, even during the war when much of it was ploughed up to provide food for the inmates of both zoos. Since then it has not only been a quiet convalescent home for sick animals but has become the centre of a conservation campaign to preserve rare ones, particularly those from unsettled parts of the world where many species are in jeopardy.

Although Whipsnade still contributes to the Zoo cupboards, food has always been a major item in the budget and by the 1970s, with over 6,600 animals of more than 1,300 species to supply, not counting those in the Insect House, the problem was enormous. In 1973 the Zoo Supplies Officer spent over £84,000 on food for Regent's Park and a further £50,000 for Whipsnade. There were comments from the public when the entrance fee went up to 95p but this compared favourably with wages and salaries a century ago when the entrance fee was 1/-. The massive shopping list for 1973 included 220 tons of hay and clover, 40 tons of carrots, 60 tons of potatoes, 60,000 lbs of cabbage, 5,000 lbs of tomatoes, 40,000 eggs and 23,000 pints of milk. Carnivorous animals got 90 tons of domesticated Australian water buffalo and horse flesh, 35,000 lbs of whiting and 12,000 lbs of sprats.

Research over the years had shown that while many animals could live reasonably healthily on a diet which might be different to that in their natural habitat, some needed 'extras' to keep them in peak health, so that monkeys are given a puffed cube of protein vitamins and minerals with their daily rations; lions have a powder containing sup-plementary vitamins tucked into their raw joints of meat, and even the blood fed to the vampire bats is laced with added vitamins.

Slowly the Zoo tried to persuade visitors not to feed the

inmates and finally in 1968 it imposed a complete ban. For many years they offered tit-bits which at times caused serious illness and even death. Stale and mouldy bread or buns upset the strongest stomachs; sandwiches left over from picnics could carry germs of colds and 'flu which affected the monkeys in particular. At one time the danger of greedy animals over-eating on food provided by visitors was so great that they had to be given a purgative before a Bank Holiday.

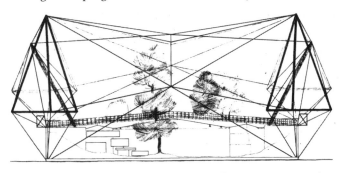

The Aviary, designed in 1965 by Lord Snowdon in association with Cedric Price and Frank Newby

Not all the food was orthodox. In one year alone the Zoo's elephants removed fourteen coats, twelve handbags, ten cameras and eight gloves as well as six return tickets to Leicester. And they even swallowed a Greek visitor's handbag containing passports and identity passes.

It was after the Second World War that the Zoo began to enter a new era of success. Newspapers and magazine features had built up before the war. In 1934 a new penguin pool had been opened – another architectural experiment. The architects, Lubetkin/Tecton, used reinforced concrete to produce a revolutionary design with sweeping 'walkways' down into the water. Scientists, keepers and public all approved. The pool was comfortable, easy to keep clean and showed the penguins off to the best advantage.

Publicity flourished under the strong personality of Julian

Huxley. The chimpanzees' tea party had become another huge attraction, while talks on pre-war Children's Hour by the Zoo Man, David Seth-Smith, stimulated more interest. In 1938 the first giant Panda, 'Ming', arrived and although all the poisonous snakes had to be destroyed and many animals evacuated to Whipsnade during the war, the public appetite for the more serious side of the Zoo had been stimulated.

In 1946 the 'gate' reached an unprecedented $2\frac{3}{4}$ million and in 1947 the Society appointed a permanent architect, F. A. P. Stengelhofen, and charged him with replanning much of the old lay-out. Like his early predecessor, Decimus Burton, he produced plans many of which were not used, but his animal hospital and quarantine station were built.

Most of his scheme was abandoned through lack of funds when, after the immediate post-war surge, attendances began to drop. In 1950 Brumas, the polar bear, brought new fortune as visits soared to nearly three million a year, but figures later fell again to below two million.

Despite this, the Council took the enlightened step of planning a New Zoo. The scientific and educational side would be strengthened and the public would be allowed in at all times during regular opening hours – even on Sunday mornings, which were still the hallowed perquisite of the Fellows. For some time there was uproar, not from the professional zoologists, but from the many laymen who paid their subscription and wanted their rights to the exclusive use of the Gardens on Sunday mornings. The Society was taken to the High Court but they eventually won their case and the public was allowed full access at last.

Led by its Honorary Secretary, Sir Solly (later Lord) Zuckerman, and encouraged by its President, Sir Landsborough Thomson, the Council appointed Sir Hugh Casson consultant architect, entrusting to him the plans for designing a New Zoo in the now thirty-six acres of Zoological Gardens.

By 1959, in association with Stengelhofen and landscape architect Peter Shepheard, he had produced an overall scheme which would transform the existing Zoo. The buildings would no longer be based on the old hit-and-miss methods of animal care which had marked much of Victorian planning through sheer lack of experience. The brief for each house could be based on past knowledge and drawn up carefully, laying out the proved principles which the design should follow to satisfy the needs of the animals and the public and to allow it to be managed simply and effectively. An example of this was the Moonlight World for mammals in the Charles Clore pavilion, where night was turned into day so that the public might see, in dim light, animals which were normally nocturnal deluded by near-darkness to come out and play in what beyond the walls of the 'cage' was daytime.

All that was needed for the New Zoo was financial backing. There was no longer a vein of rich gentlemen to provide resources. An appeal to the Fellows failed, but many philanthropists came to the rescue, realising the value of the Zoo, not only as a London attraction but for its scientific work. In particular Sir Charles Clore, Sir Michael Sobell and Jack Cotton contributed handsomely. Major foundations including the Wellcome, the Nuffield and the Ford groups helped to establish new research institutes.

The Cotton Terraces, designed by Peter Shepheard, were built alongside the canal in the northern section of the Gardens to provide new homes for the zebras, giraffes, camels, deer and antelope. Stengelhofen and Shepheard combined to produce a whole scheme of indoor accommodation and outdoor 'plains', but retained Burton's original building, still ideal for its purpose of housing giraffes. A new bridge designed by Sir Hugh Casson was built across the canal and a landing stage established to allow visitors to arrive by boat in the centre of the Gardens. Lord Snowdon designed a unique aviary, where the public might walk above waterfalls and rockeries with sacred ibises nesting round them, egrets and heron drifting overhead. A new elephant house was built from Casson's plans, a strange honeycomb complex with roofs like the raised trunks of a herd of elephants. The rhinos share its almost lunar setting. Later Sir Michael Sobell financed new

The Elephant House by Sir Hugh Casson

monkey and ape pavilions where, as a temporary measure, the giant pandas Ching-Ching and Chia-Chia were first housed.

Two more major developments of the 1960s and 70s were the establishment of the Nuffield and Wellcome Research buildings. The Wellcome Institute of Comparative Physiology was opened in 1962 as a centre for studying animal breeding and reproduction. Its findings were to be of value to zoos all over the world.

The Nuffield Institute of Comparative Medicine, set up in 1964, was to concentrate on comparative studies in pathology, biochemistry, radiology and infectious diseases. Its work has been supported not only by the Wellcome Trust but by the Medical Research Council, the Natural Environment Research Council and the World Health Organisation among others.

Apart from helping the Zoo to keep its animals healthy in captivity, its work is leading to a better understanding of the diseases of wild and domestic animals as well as of man himself. This can range from preventing bone disease in monkeys to helping in a study of coronary thrombosis or mental health in human beings.

In the 1970s, for the first time, the Society applied to the Government for financial help towards its rebuilding and was granted a capital loan for five years. By now it was contributing on a massive scale to world knowledge of zoology and had launched a new Year Book of international value, particularly to zoo managers. It had a wide programme of education enjoyed by thousands of schoolchildren, teachers, students and graduates as well as a thriving 'XYZ' Club for over 4,000 young naturalists. Closest links had been set up with radio and television and all the news media.

By its 150th year, the Zoo would be unrecognisable to its founders. The concept of raising useful stock for country estates had vanished. Successors of many of the original patrons were still supporting the Society – in 1970 the Queen donated a family of beavers, gift of the Hudson's Bay Company, both carrying on with past tradition. In 1974, the Chinese Government presented the people of Britain with the two giant pandas, Ching-Ching and Chia-Chia, which passed into the care of the Society.

The whole purpose of the Zoo, a century and a half on, is aimed towards education, conservation, comparative biology and relating the study of every aspect of animal life to other branches of science.

Already, serious thought is being given to whether a Zoo is justifiable and the defence rests not on grounds of public entertainment but on its uses for education and research, which could ultimately benefit both animals and humans all over the world. In these the Zoological Society of London carries on the tradition for which it was founded and which, despite its vicissitudes, in principle it has maintained since its opening day.

Griffon Vulture, by Mrs J. Gould, 1873

Sir Stamford Raffles by G. F. Joseph

Sir Humphrey Davy after Sir Thomas Lawrence

Chimpanzee or African Orang-Utan, by G. Scharf, 1835

Cabee   Omar   ZAIDA   MABROUK   SELIM   GIRRAFAH   Abdallah   M Thibaut

Giraffes with their Arab attendants, by G. Scharf, 1835

The Bear Pit, by G. Scharf, 1835

The Llama House, by G. Scharf, 1835

Spotted Owlets and Jungle Owlets, by C. F. Sharpe, 1885

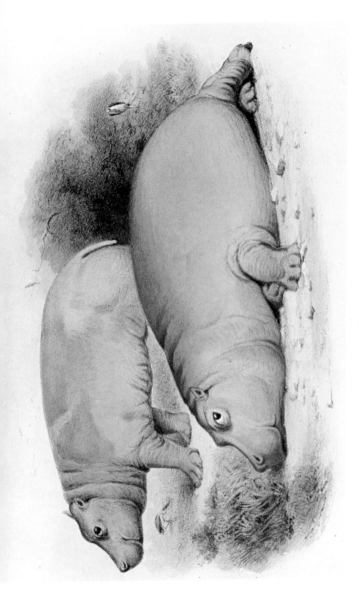

Two Hippos, by Joseph Wolf, from a sketch made in Cairo in 1849. The hippo in the foreground is Obaysch.

Taphozous Bat by Theodore Cantor, 1845

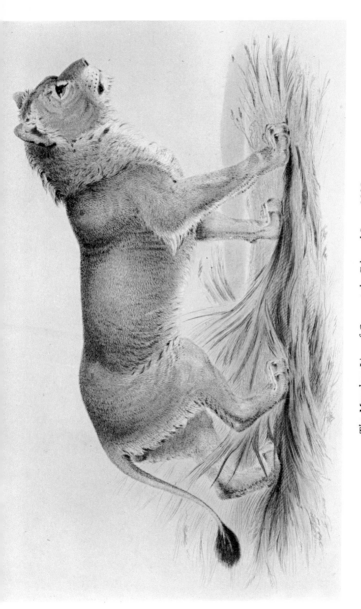

The Maneless Lion of Guzerat, by Edward Lear, 1835

View from the Emu House, by James Hakewill 1831

General view of the Zoological Gardens in 1835

Charles F. Flower

The Broadwalk with Elephants, by Charles F. Flower

Cover for a song sheet in 1882

贈　給
英國人民

中華人民共和國政府贈

A Gift to the British People
With the compliments
of the Government of the
People's Republic of China
1974

*Portrait of Ching Ching and Chia Chia, the Giant Pandas presented
to the Zoological Society of London in October 1974.*

Admit ....

TO THE GARDENS

ZOOLOGI

Cha...

Each Person to pay One Shillin